WHISTLING BOMBS AND BUMPY TRAINS

the *Life-Story* of

ANNA NIXON

by

Betty M. Hockett

To Gary —
Betty M. Hockett

GEORGE FOX PRESS

600 EAST THIRD STREET • NEWBERG, OREGON 97132

To
ELIZABETH ROSE
whose namesake-grandmother promises to pray for
her every day while she grows up with her
missionary parents in a faraway place.

WHISTLING BOMBS AND BUMPY TRAINS

The LIFE-STORY of Anna Nixon

© 1989 George Fox Press
Library of Congress Catalog Card Number: 89-84572
ISBN: 0-94370-15-5

Cover by Jannelle Loewen

Litho in U.S.A. by The Barclay Press, Newberg, Oregon

CONTENTS

Chapter 1

'WHERE'S ANNA?'

"I want to go, too," said three-year-old Anna Nixon one summer day in 1920. "I like to do things with you and your friends." She danced around her older brothers and sisters, waiting eagerly for their invitation.

Instead of inviting, Hazel grumbled. "Does Annie have to go with us?"

"She'll only slow us down," Ray muttered.

"Annie can never keep up," Carl said.

Their oldest sister, Laura, added, "Who cares if she comes? I don't. We don't have to pay attention to her."

The four oldest children rushed off to meet their friends. The Nixon's large Colorado farm made a perfect place for summer fun. First they played hide-and-seek in the cornfield. After that they ran to the orchard to jump up and grab apricots off the trees. The fruit tasted good. Later the seeds made wonderful ammunition as the children chased each other through the cucumber patch.

Anna skipped along behind, never quite catching up.

Next, the older Nixons and their friends nibbled on young carrots and chewed the sweet, juicy sugar cane. They chattered and giggled as they straddled the fence by the barnyard, noisy with calves, colts, pigs, and chickens.

In all the fun, no one thought to pay attention to Anna. They didn't realize she hadn't climbed on the fence with them. At four o'clock the friends said good-bye and the Nixons trooped back to their house.

"Where's Annie?" their mother asked.

Laura, Hazel, Carl, and Ray looked around. No Anna. They glanced at one another.

"She was right behind us," said Carl.

"I saw her in the orchard once," said Laura.

"But where is she now?" Mrs. Nixon demanded.

"Do you think we ought to go look for her?" Hazel asked.

"Yes, I do. Even though her legs can't run as fast as yours, she ought to be here by now." Mrs. Nixon gave instructions. Carl and Ray started one direction while Hazel and Laura went the other.

Just as her worried mother decided to get more help, Anna stumbled around the corner of the house.

"Mama? Mama?" she cried. "I...I'm so tired...just awful tired, Mama. All over I'm tired." Tears made muddy trails down her cheeks.

Fannie Nixon scooped Anna up and cuddled her close. "Oh, little Annie, I'm so thankful you're all right."

Two hours later, Anna appeared far from being all right.

"Mama, come quick! Annie's acting funny!" Hazel yelled.

"She's shaking all over!" shouted Carl.

Mother flew into action the minute she saw Anna. She called to her husband. "Fern, Annie's having a convulsion."

Fern Nixon hurried to see. So did Grandma Van Gieson, Fannie's mother who had come to help at the birth of the sixth Nixon baby. After one look, Anna's father announced he would saddle the horse and go for the doctor. That meant a 40-mile ride to Elkhart, Kansas.

Grandma immediately got out all the home remedies she could find. She did everything she knew to stop the convulsions. At last Anna's muscles relaxed their unnatural twitching. Grandma Van Gieson had saved Anna's life.

The doctor arrived early the next day. He quickly stuck a thermometer into Anna's mouth and listened to her heart. While he peered into her eyes his expert fingers flexed her arms and legs.

Looking at the thermometer, the doctor said quietly, "All I can say is, you had better give thanks to God that Anna is still alive."

No one ever knew for sure why Anna had been so sick.

*　　*　　*

One day someone said to Mr. and Mrs. Nixon, "What a big family you have. And poor, too."

Fern and Fannie Nixon looked at their seven children. "We're not poor," they said. "We have lots of love and happiness along with our hard work." The Nixon children always had plenty of milk to drink and good chicken for many evening suppers. They wore clothes with patches, but they had all they needed. They saw sincerity, honesty, dependability, hard work, justice, and love in the lives of their parents.

The Nixon family lived far away from any church. Mrs. Nixon made sure, though, to take her children to Sunday school at the country schoolhouse whenever possible.

Anna entered first grade just before her fifth birthday, bouncing on the horse's back to and from school each day. How could anyone have known then that someday she would bounce along on bumpy trains more than halfway around the world?

*　　*　　*

One summer afternoon, seven-year-old Anna leaned against the sturdy elm tree in front of the Nixon farmhouse. She had serious thoughts about

God as she slowly pulled hunks of bark off the tree. *There's something I need to do if I am to be a Christian. I don't want to go to hell. Only Jesus can help me.*

Anna walked away from the tree and into the house. "How old were you when you were saved?" she asked her mother.

"Eight years old," Fannie Nixon replied.

I'm only seven, Anna thought. *That means I have one more year to go.*

As it turned out, she didn't ask Jesus to be her Savior until three years after that. An evangelist came for revival meetings at the Prairie Dell School, and Mrs. Nixon took with her the children who wanted to go. Anna heard the preacher say, "All who wish to be saved should come forward to kneel and pray." Anna felt too bashful at first, but when Hazel walked to the front, Anna did too.

Starting at that moment, she planned to do exactly what God wanted.

*   *   *

As Anna started the eighth grade, the Nixon family moved into the town of Vilas, Colorado. Right away Anna discovered a Friends church nearby.

She went to that church every Sunday for several months. Then she became discouraged and stopped going regularly.

*   *   *

The day Anna graduated from the red, brick high school, Ellis and Ferne Cook arrived in Vilas. They had come to pastor the Friends Church. The Cooks began to notice that Anna sometimes turned up for Sunday school but seldom stayed for the worship service. They started to pray for her. Soon the pastor and his wife became Anna's special friends. They persuaded her to attend both Sunday school and the worship service every Sunday.

Anna knew before long that God wanted her to be a missionary. She found it hard to say, "Yes."

One night at church, God reminded Anna she had not really been living as a Christian for a long time. *I'm sorry, Lord,* she prayed. *I will give myself completely to You from now on.* With the next breath she added, *And, Lord, I will be a missionary.*

That decision changed Anna's life.

Anna (on the left) with her brothers and sisters

Chapter 2

LEAVING HOME

"Anna, what in the world makes you want to be a missionary?" people asked.

"One day God spoke to me and called me to serve Him as a missionary. I can never doubt this call from God," she explained.

Anna knew she would need to go to college. "There's no money for me to go now, though," she told Ellis and Ferne Cook.

She got a job, and after a few months she had saved enough to make definite plans. The Cooks suggested, "We're planning to drive to Cleveland, Ohio. We'll be glad to take you with us so you can enroll in Cleveland Bible College."

Anna had already read about this school. "Yes," she replied, "I believe that's where I should prepare to be a missionary."

Some of their friends laughed when they heard about Ellis and Ferne's plan. "You'll never make it far in that old Model T Ford," they predicted.

But, the car and its passengers made it safely to Cleveland.

Anna inquired at the college office about where she would live. The secretary told her, "We have arranged for you to work as a maid for a family. You'll get your room and meals free in their home and three dollars a week besides."

Ellis then said, "Come on, we'll take you to your new home." They piled back into the Ford. At the next corner, the traffic signal turned red. The car shook and made a dreadful noise as the motor quit. Ellis tried over and over again to get the car started. It sat like a rock.

"Well, that's the end of this car," he said, shaking his head.

"Praise the Lord it got us this far," said Ferne with a hearty laugh.

*   *   *

One of the first students to welcome Anna happened to be Milton Coleman. "Several college students who work in the city come to our house on Thursday afternoons," he said. "Why don't you come, too?"

As things turned out, many years later Milton welcomed Anna into another new situation far from Ohio. But that first year in Cleveland, Anna went to the Coleman home every Thursday afternoon—her regular time off from work as a maid. There she met many students, including Rebecca, engaged to marry Milton.

Anna enjoyed the routine of work, college classes, and study. Even so, she constantly felt homesick. Often she counted the ticks of the clock. Each tick made her think, *I'm that much nearer the time when I can go home again and see my family.*

At last the time came for graduation. The senior women decided to wear white shoes, something Anna did not have. She didn't have money to buy any, either. After she prayed about it, she thought, *I have brown shoes I could wear. I should be content with those. After all, people in many places of the world don't have even one pair of shoes. Yes, Lord, I'm willing to wear the brown shoes.*

A few days later Anna received an unexpected gift of money. She used it to buy several things she really needed. Then, with the leftover dollars, she bought new white shoes.

*   *   *

A few months later, Anna asked Kansas Yearly Meeting of Friends about their missionary work in Africa. "We're not sending out unmarried missionaries," the mission board replied. Anna knew she would have to wait until God showed her where He wanted her to go.

Sometime later she applied to Ohio Yearly Meeting of Friends for work in India or China. Soon she received the answer, "Please meet with our mission board."

Men and women on the mission board questioned Anna thoroughly. "Can you lead people to Jesus? Will you get along with others? Can you take advice? Are you cheerful and kind?"

A while after the interview, they told her, "Everyone who knows you speaks highly of you. We like you, too. We want you to be one of our missionaries to India."

The president of the mission board prepared a cablegram to notify the Friends missionaries in India. Anna felt like shouting when she saw what it said: *Nixon to arrive in India October, 1940.*

With World War II underway in Europe, Anna found it hard to get her passport and visa. In fact, when October came, she still didn't have all of these papers necessary for entering India. "It's too dangerous to travel now in wartime, anyway," the mission board said.

Three months later, Anna decided, *I'll wait and go next October. Surely everything will be in order by that time.*

So, even though the war had not yet ended a year later, Anna boarded the large ship, the *U.S.S. President Grant.* On November 9, 1941, she watched as the buildings of San Francisco got smaller and smaller. "It won't be long now until I'll be in India," she said.

At least that's what she thought.

Chapter 3

BLACKOUTS AND AIR RAIDS

Swollen waves rolled the *U.S.S. President Grant* this way and that. Anna's stomach rose and fell along with the ship.

By the time the ship docked in Honolulu, however, Anna felt better. She signed up to tour the pineapple cannery and famous Waikiki Beach. A few days later she began to worry. *We've been here too long; I wonder why the delay.*

"We're concerned about the war being so close," a government official explained. "We must make sure a destroyer and a cruiser can travel in convoy with you. Once you leave here, you need to observe a complete blackout at night. That means *no* lights."

Finally the *U.S.S. President Grant* and its escorts left Honolulu for the Philippine Islands. The ships arrived safely in Manila on December 4.

Anna and other passengers went sight-seeing about the city. Each day they watched for a notice of when the ship would continue its journey.

11

One morning Anna sat down as usual to breakfast in the ship's dining room. The juicy, pale yellow grapefruit half looked tasty sitting on the plate before her. After a prayer, she took up her spoon and started to eat.

Suddenly, an unseen voice announced on the ship's loudspeaker, "This morning the Japanese bombed Pearl Harbor!" The dining room atmosphere shattered like a dish falling to the floor.

Anna stopped chewing. Her right hand dangled the spoon in midair. "Pearl Harbor bombed! That means war, and we're in the center of the trouble!" she exclaimed.

Spoons and forks dropped with a clatter and everyone began to talk at once. "The Japanese will surely come this way next.... They'll likely bomb Manila tonight, and the port is the first place they'll hit.... We'd better leave the ship."

"Some of us don't have any other place to go," Anna said.

Grapefruit, toast, eggs, and coffee sat untouched. Chairs scraped the floor as passengers hastily pushed away from the table.

The eating area emptied quickly.

In less than an hour, many of the people lugged their suitcases down the gangplank to hunt for a safer place on shore. Anna stayed aboard the ship.

Big bombers roared over Manila Bay that night, exactly as the passengers had feared. In spite of the dreadful noise and the blackout, Anna and ten others gathered in the ship's darkened lounge. Her eyes circled this group of missionaries: five, like herself, going away from the United States for the first time—five more who already had been to India at least once. Light from one flashlight made everything look strange and scary.

The noise overhead made conversation difficult. As best they could, however, the eleven huddled together to read Scripture verses and pray together. Their togetherness spread courage among them. "We want to stay close to God no matter what happens," they agreed.

A few hours later, Anna crawled into her bunk. She thought about her four brothers. *Will they have to go to war?* she wondered.

The waves swooshed against the side of the ship. All at once the scream of a siren jarred Anna out of her thoughts. Someone ran along the passage yelling, "Air raid! Everyone down to the hold!"

Anna jumped out of her bunk and dashed to the stifling, dirty hold at the bottom of the ship. Sometime later the all-clear signal rang out, and the passengers felt their way back along the dark passages to their rooms.

Two more times that night the siren made Anna scramble down to the ship's hold. Each time, she could see where bombs had fallen on the other side of the bay. The area, brilliant with flames, looked like a giant bonfire. "It's sad that war has come to Manila," Anna said.

The next day the little group of missionaries had orders to leave the ship. "Where shall we go?" they asked each other.

Someone from Manila told them, "The Oriente Hotel has rooms left—the only place that does." But it's in a dangerous part of the city."

Anna hurriedly packed a suitcase. She and the ten others climbed into the horse-drawn carriages and rattled off down the street. They looked back at their trunks and suitcases left on Pier Seven. "Will we ever see our possessions again?" Anna asked.

The eleven American missionaries quickly settled into the Oriente Hotel. "We should send cablegrams to our mission boards," someone suggested. "They need to know what's happening."

"What shall we say?" one asked.

They spent the next few minutes talking it over. Finally they all agreed to send the same message. Each cablegram contained just two words, *Delayed, Manila!*

* * *

"You must not have any lights on at night," warned the owner of the hotel. "American soldiers live in the buildings directly across the street. Even one light would show the Japanese bombers what's down here."

"The Japanese bomb the Americans and the Americans bomb the Japanese," said Anna. "It's all wrong! Love is God's way, not hate."

14

Anna and the ten other missionaries often spent the long dark evenings together in one room. They prayed, "Lord, please send a ship to take us on to India."

At first Anna slept in her clothes. The blaring air raid siren sent the hotel residents running down the steps to the protection of the hallway below several times each night.

During the days, Anna and the others visited with the American soldiers. The missionaries stood on one side of the iron fence that separated the hotel from the army barracks. The young men lined the other side. They talked about many things, and sometimes they admitted to being lonely and afraid, just like the missionaries. Anna, and the others, too, gladly prayed with the soldiers.

One evening when Anna trudged back inside the hotel, she silently prayed, *Thank You, God. You've given us this opportunity to help others here in Manila.*

*   *   *

"Christmas will soon be here, even though we're in the midst of war," Anna said one day. "Jesus came to earth to be the Prince of Peace. We must remember His birthday."

She and another missionary, Dr. Evelyn Witthoff, bought a small Christmas tree and carried it back to the hotel. Others helped decorate it with silver tinsel, bright balls, and artificial snow. A special peace seemed to hover over the hotel lobby. Many people came in for a closer look.

On Christmas Eve, a man stood in the hotel doorway. He looked out at the ruined city and said, "'Tis the night before Christmas, and all through the town the sirens are shrieking and bombs falling down."

"But look!" exclaimed Anna, stepping up beside the man. "We can see so much more than just the heaps of rubble. Did you notice that glorious red and gold sunset this evening? And see how the stars twinkle tonight? They look especially bright in the blackout."

Seeing the two standing there, a passerby stopped. Soon others gathered, looking at the stars, too. Someone began to hum a favorite Christmas carol. Another added words to the tune. "Joy to the world! The Lord is come: Let earth receive her King...." Before long, everyone sang the comforting words.

The Prince of Peace Himself is here this very moment, thought Anna.

*　　*　　*

The Americans heard the whine of airplane motors all day on December 26. Anna lost track of how many times she rolled to safety under the bed.

The next day huge fires broke out nearby. Anna and the other missionaries prepared to leave in a hurry. "But there's no way out," said Anna. "The city is burning up."

A man explained to the group, "The American soldiers have gone, but they've done their best to protect Manila. They blew up the oil dumps so the Japanese couldn't use the oil in their fight against the United States. They set fire to the bridges to keep the Japanese soldiers from coming in to capture the city."

Hot, dense smoke shut out the sun for the next three days. On one of those days, Anna received a cablegram from the United States. She nervously tore open the envelope and read the message aloud. "Anna, through fire I will be with thee. Isaiah 43:2. Signed, James Tatsch, President, Christian Endeavor Society, First Friends Church, Cleveland, Ohio."

As the fires continued to burn all around, Anna spoke with new courage. "We're not alone, even in the fire." A long time after that, Anna found out her cable had been the last message to come from the United States before the American Embassy in Manila closed down.

*　　*　　*

In spite of everything the American soldiers had done to keep the Japanese away, they flooded into the city anyway.

The Manila shopkeepers knew what that meant. They told the Filipinos, "Take anything you want. The Japanese will get it if you don't." They threw open the doors of their shops and people rushed to gather whatever they could carry.

The missionaries leaned out their hotel windows and watched people hurry by. At first they laughed at one man with a dozen hats crammed on his head. Bundles of clothes filled his arms. Suddenly it didn't seem funny.

"He's wearing your hats!" Anna shouted to one missionary.

"That man over there has my books!" yelled another.

The next day they read these headlines in the newspaper: *Baggage at Pier Seven Looted and Burned.*

*   *   *

To make the time pass faster the next afternoon, Anna sat on the floor in her hotel room typing. All at once she heard heavy steps in the hall. Then her door jerked open, banging against the wall. Her hands instantly froze in their typing position as she stared at the sharp point of a bayonet held just a few feet from her face. A uniformed Japanese soldier stood boldly in the doorway.

Anna gasped! As she looked along the bayonet to the gun strapped to it, fear squeezed at her like cold fingers. The soldier who held the gun said something Anna could not understand. After several seconds that seemed like hours, she discovered he had ordered her to follow him to the hotel lobby.

The soldiers forced the Americans to stand outside in a line for the next two hours. They arranged and rearranged the lineup and nervously searched everyone again and again. *Will they just go on counting us or go ahead and shoot us?* Anna wondered. Fear still made her feel icy cold.

Finally one soldier read instructions to them. "We are taking you away for three days. Get things you will need for three days and be back in three minutes."

Everyone quickly obeyed. Anna came back downstairs with a suitcase, her typewriter, and one blanket.

The soldiers transported the Americans across town and forced them to remain in an auditorium at the University of the Philippines. More Americans, along with British citizens, joined the group of captives. The next three days passed slowly and uncomfortably with almost no food for anyone.

During the afternoon of January 6, the Japanese soldiers again counted everyone several times. Then, finished with that ordeal, they loaded ten Americans at a time into a station wagon and headed out across town. Anna ended up with nine people she did not know.

All at once she felt more alone than ever in her life before. She had no idea where her missionary friends would end up. Would she ever be able to find them?

In a short while, the station wagon drove through an open gate into the grounds of Santo Tomas University. Anna and the nine others got out and walked toward the main building. It seemed large and luxurious compared to where they had been for the last three days.

Anna heard the lock on the gate click shut behind them. She looked back at the guards who stood sternly at both sides of the entrance. At that moment the truth hit Anna as hard as if she had run full speed into the brick wall.

I am a prisoner!

The dark hole in the bottom of the ship where passengers went during blackouts

Chapter 4

A HOPELESS SITUATION

Anna stumbled into the main building of Santo Tomas University. She looked about, feeling weak and helpless from lack of food or sleep. "I am no longer free," she murmured.

She did, however, have the freedom to hunt for her friends. Three hours later she found them in a classroom. "Anna!" they exclaimed amid hugs. "We prayed we would somehow find each other."

"Welcome to our living quarters," said one woman, already starting to tidy up the room. The others set to work, too, brushing away the dusty cobwebs and scraping garbage into a corner.

While Anna and her friends worked, an officer chalked 45 on the door. "Is that the number of our room?" someone asked.

"It means 45 women will occupy this room," the officer replied gruffly.

It ended up that 47 women and children crowded in before the end of the day. Overtired mothers spoke crossly to their children. Frightened boys and girls cried. No one had any privacy, and all had to walk down a long hall to the bathroom.

"We can be thankful we have a good supply of water," said Anna, trying to be cheerful.

That night she and six other women lay down side by side on the floor in one corner of the room. They felt too exhausted to worry that their stomachs churned and growled with hunger. The next morning they woke up even hungrier. Swollen, itchy mosquito bites all over their bodies added to the misery. Anna counted 27 bites on just her left hand.

The first few days at Santo Tomas, the prisoners wandered about, confused and uncertain. Kind Filipinos outside the big locked gate brought food. A few weeks later they also supplied mattresses, sheets, blankets, pillows, and mosquito nets.

Anna and the six ladies who slept beside her every night received one big mosquito net and two mattresses. They turned the mattresses sideways. That way, each woman had 23 inches of space to herself, even though both feet hung over the edge.

As they became more organized, the prisoners thought of the days ahead. What about school for the children? Should they plant gardens? They also discussed recreation, religious services, and more living space.

Some said, "The Americans will soon return in a grand victory. We don't need to make a lot of plans." A few leaders did, anyway. No one knew then how important those plans would be.

The prisoners tried to be thoughtful of one another, and everyone had several jobs. One work crew planted a garden. Anna had no idea the vegetables, and even the weeds, would eventually help save her life.

The prisoners established classes for all ages. Students had to ignore the noisy people milling about, and classroom sites changed often. Anna worked hard on the committee that planned religious services and other worthwhile activities.

They scheduled regular church services, including Sunday school classes. Sometimes the Japanese officials came to the services, too. Eventually someone found a folding organ that provided a huffy-puffy accompaniment to singing. Several singers, including Anna, formed a choir and also a women's chorus. They performed inspiring music such as the "Hallelujah Chorus."

Some of the university officials, as well as others, donated books for the prisoners. Social activities and sports events helped take up time. Doctors and nurses announced regular clinic hours.

Anna discovered a prisoner named Dr. Wilson Hume, who had been a missionary in India. He helped her study the Hindi language. Before long, Anna could read a few words in the Hindi New Testament she had borrowed from a friend.

Santo Tomas Internment Camp took on the appearance of a small city, its 4,000 residents busy much of the time. Restlessness and unhappiness took over, however, in spite of everyone's activity. No one could ever be alone. Loud talking in the daytime and snoring at night became nearly unbearable. Food supplies dwindled. Worms and weevils mingled in the rice and beans.

Selfishness began to show up in words and actions. Authorities could hardly keep order in the camp. Responsible people tried to make a few simple rules. That, too, soon got out of hand when rules appeared for everything: when to talk, when to be quiet, how to stand in line, how to walk down the hall, when to take a nap.

Prisoners grew angry and complained about the rules. "Even though rules are hard, they will help us have a better life here in the camp," Anna said.

She appreciated people who showed the love of Jesus in spite of the difficulties. "Jesus told His followers, 'I am the Way,'" Anna said. "He still is the Way even now. We must follow His way. We must show His love in our actions."

Day by day the weeks went by. *We're in a world at war*, thought Anna sadly. *Will I ever get to India? Will I even get out of prison camp?* She longed for contact with her family. She felt discouraged and distressed with the news about the war.

The first year in prison ended with Anna and everyone else hoping freedom would come soon.

Camp life had been bad, but they had no idea it would get worse.

*   *   *

Anna did all she could to find things to cheer the drab days. Quiet early morning walks alone under the trees helped. She enjoyed her daily work as typing teacher and secretary at the hospital. Every few days she checked two or three books out of the camp library. Anna looked forward to teaching her Sunday school class.

The high school girls—all prisoners—who came to Anna's Sunday school class became the joy of her life. She had no materials to use in teaching so she made her own. She couldn't have guessed that in a few years she would do the same thing for many more people.

Then, changes came about that cheered the prisoners for a time. Filipino vendors received new permission to bring their wares into the camp. At the same time, Chinese people in Manila made secret arrangements to loan money to the prisoners. "You can pay it back after the war," they said.

The prisoners used their loans to buy extra food from the vendors. The peanuts, coconuts, limes, cucumbers, and other fruits and vegetables cost a lot, but they tasted good.

Another change specifically helped Anna and her roommates. They got individual beds made of wooden planks. Each bed had a slick straw mat-

25

tress and a mosquito net. Anna rolled off onto the floor the first night she slept alone. "I'm not used to so much space or such a slick mattress," she laughingly said the next morning.

The weeks hurried by, and Anna celebrated her second Christmas in the prison camp. Each prisoner received a packet of food from the British Red Cross. "Look at this," said Anna happily. She inspected the canned meat, jam, preserved butter, chocolate, cheese, coffee, raisins, bouillon, crackers, and special vitamin pills. Anna managed to make these treats last nearly a year.

*   *   *

On her way to work at the hospital one day, Anna saw a mountain of packages stacked against a building. "They're sorted and arranged alphabetically," someone said.

Anna dashed to the "N" line. She listened eagerly for her name. When she heard "Nixon," she shouted, "I'm here!" and pushed forward for her package. The return address had been written in her mother's handwriting. It looked more wonderful to Anna than anything she had seen for a long time. "My first contact from home since I left 29 months ago," she said to anyone who cared to hear.

Clothes, washcloths, a towel, pencils, a comb, buttons, and handkerchiefs tumbled out of the box. She thanked God that He had arranged for her to receive these items at the exact time she needed them.

*   *   *

Some of the Japanese officials seemed friendly to the prisoners. But suddenly, the one who had been the kindest left Santo Tomas. The prisoners immediately felt the effect.

From then on, the Japanese military government took command of the camp. The officers quickly made new rules. No Filipinos could come into the camp, not even to sell food. No prisoners had permission to go out. Roll call became a military routine, sometimes lasting for two hours.

These Japanese soldiers in our camp seem so young, thought Anna. They looked almost as thin as the prisoners, and Anna noticed they also planted gardens. Sometimes she smiled at the soldiers and they smiled at her. *We don't hate each other*, she thought. *This war is senseless and wrong*.

The food supply got lower and lower since nothing came in from the outside. The gardens helped, but Anna and the others still did not have nearly enough to eat. Serious illnesses broke out among the children and among the adults as well.

As the months went by, just staying alive took all of Anna's strength. Food became the main topic of conversation everywhere, even at Bible studies.

God asked Anna one day, *Will you still believe in Me if no food comes?* She couldn't answer right away. For a long time she thought about herself and her problems. In the end, she could truthfully reply, *Yes, God, even though I die I will trust in You.*

Groups of prisoners continued to meet for Bible study, devotions, and prayer. "Christ is all we have now," Anna said. "He is more precious than ever."

After awhile, American planes regularly flew over Manila. They shot at Japanese targets. The Japanese shot at the American planes. Air raids, with the ear-splitting sounds of bombs whistling through the air, filled the days and nights.

Every day many prisoners died from disease and starvation. Illness left most of the others so weak they could barely move. *Will most of us die before freedom comes?* Anna wondered.

Then, late one night, American soldiers broke through the walls of the camp in their heavy army tanks. They immediately took charge that day, February 3, 1945. Anna sang "The Star Spangled Banner" and "God Bless America" along with everyone else. Tears wet her cheeks as the red, white, and blue American flag fluttered gracefully at the top of the flagpole.

It's all over! she thought.

Soon she knew differently. After all, Santo Tomas still lay in the war zone, and the fighting had not ended.

Chapter 5

THE END OF MORE THAN 1,000 DAYS

Anna's joy faded fast as the fighting went on. Shells and bombs whistled and exploded all around the prison camp. Planes blew apart while in flight, then crashed to the ground in flashes of fire and smoke. Young soldiers from both sides died. Inside the walls, people still didn't have enough food. Many more died of starvation.

American soldiers brought mail to the prisoners. A letter from Anna's parents told about her brother Vern: *He's missing in action.*

On the morning of February 7, artillery shells landed on the buildings where Anna had lived for more than three years. Walls caved in. Glass flew about like drops of rain. Several of her close friends died instantly. Others survived but would live with horrible scars for the rest of their lives.

Ten days later, those terrible times drew to a close.

Kitchen workers obtained new food supplies. Anna and the others had bread for the first time in three years. They ate and ate, all the while talking over the joys and tragedies they had experienced together. The extra food helped Anna gain weight, going from 95 to 110 pounds.

Anna celebrated Easter before leaving camp in April. As she strolled among the buildings once more, she thought of Jesus who had died and risen again. She cried at the memory of the young American soldiers who had died almost in front of her eyes. Anna also thought a lot about Vern and about Frank, her youngest brother, who served on a submarine somewhere in the Pacific Ocean.

Anna's mind then turned to the Japanese men who died when American guns had blasted their airplanes out of the sky. They, too, had families at home, crying because their loved ones would not return from war. Jesus had given His life for them, too.

Because of this war, life can never be the same for anyone, she told herself. Anna took one last look at the place she had called "home" for 1,201 days. She would never forget God's faithfulness throughout those dreadful days in prison.

The time had come to leave all that behind. Anna turned and walked toward the ship that would take her home to family and friends.

* * *

The Nixons welcomed Anna back. Their reunion had sad times, though, because they knew by then that Vern would never be with them again. Guns had shot his plane down over Yugoslavia, and his body had been buried there.

Anna took time to rest and gain strength. After a few weeks, she went out to speak in several churches, telling about her prison experiences. She also wrote about them in her first book, which she titled *Delayed, Manila*.

"Do you still want to be a missionary?" people asked.

"Oh yes," Anna quickly replied. "I hope to start for India as soon as possible. I want to tell how Jesus took care of me and how He can save people from sin if they ask Him. If only one Hindu child comes to Jesus because of my work, it will be worthwhile."

One day in March, 1946, Anna boarded a troop ship in San Francisco and once again began the long journey to India. About a month later the ship docked in the Manila harbor. Parts of sunken ships poked up through the water. The shrill whistle of bombs echoed in Anna's mind. The clocktower of Santo Tomas University, as seen in the distance, looked like a finger pointing upward.

I lived close to that tower for a long time, she thought. *We were in terribly close quarters with not enough of anything. I'm glad peace has finally come.*

A few weeks later, on the day before Easter, Anna saw India for the first time.

She paced the deck impatiently as the officials checked everyone's baggage. Suddenly, she heard, "Anna Nixon! There's someone down on the pier calling for you."

Anna ran to the railing. "Milton Coleman!" she shouted in surprise. She had never forgotten that day in Cleveland when he had welcomed her to college. Since then, he and Rebecca had arrived in India as Friends missionaries.

Anna and Milton hollered back and forth. "Where are we staying here in Calcutta?" Anna asked.

"Dr. and Mrs. Hume want you to go to their house."

"Really? God is so good!" she exclaimed at the thought of seeing her Hindi language teacher once again. "I haven't seen them since they left Santo Tomas. And to think I'll be in their home here!"

* * *

Milton accompanied Anna on the 36-hour train trip from Calcutta to Harpalpur in Central India. From there they went by lorry the extra 19 miles to Nowgong. As their bus came to a stop, Milton said, "Here we are!" Just then Anna saw the sign hanging on a gatepost: American Friends Mission.

The next instant she bounded off the bus and into the arms of Rebecca Coleman, Alena Calkins, Norma Freer, and Elizabeth Earle. Anna and these Friends missionaries all laughed and talked at the same time.

After two welcoming services, Rebecca Coleman told Anna, "Tomorrow we'll begin the two-day train ride up north to Landour. We'll all be there in language study for two months."

These first two train rides began the list of hundreds of such trips Anna would take during the next 34 years. She would spend days at a time bumping along on hard board seats or standing when she couldn't find room to sit. Heat, dust, smoke, and noise coming in the open windows would often wear her out. It would be many years before Anna could travel on an air-conditioned train in India.

Seeing the steep and rugged Himalayan peaks from the train this first time, Anna gasped at their beauty. "They remind me of the mountains in Colorado," she said.

She couldn't get over the startling view from the hillsides of Landour, 7,000 feet above sea level. "It's like looking down from an airplane," she said. "Everything in the valley looks so small." Rivers threaded their way to the plains below. Mountains topped with snow-hats stood tall behind the tiny villages. Evening sunsets glowed with pink and gold. After dark, lights in the valley sparkled like jewels against black velvet.

"This must be the prettiest place on earth," Anna said. She especially enjoyed the flowers. All sizes of pink, red, and yellow roses grew against the walls of Bethany Cottage, her home for now. Pansies, nasturtiums, and Canterbury bells added color to other cottages also perched along the cliffs. Many times in the years ahead, Anna would go to Landour and Bethany Cottage to escape the sickening summer heat of the plains.

*　　*　　*

June 15, 1946

Dear Mother and Dad,

Wherever we go, it's up or down. Landour is a place of extremes: high mountains, low valleys, cold and hot weather, rain and sunshine. When it rains, clouds roll up and down like window shades. Heavy fog drifts through the doors into the house. Rain sounds as if someone turned on a powerful water faucet.

Love,
Anna

Anna gradually got used to the ups and downs from home to school and back again. To get to the market, she had to walk even farther down the hill. Sometimes on Sunday, she and the others made the twenty-minute walk down the hill to the service at Woodstock School. It took forty minutes to go back up to Bethany Cottage afterward. Other Sundays, they puffed up the hill to the English church and back down to the cottage later.

Anna's days soon followed a regular routine. She headed up the hill every morning at nine o'clock for Hindi language classes. Soon after noon she walked back down for lunch and study time. As she memorized words and sentences, she thought, *I'm glad I learned some Hindi in prison.*

Rebecca Coleman said many years later, "Anna knew how to concentrate. She could knit, take part in a group conversation, and study Hindi all at the same time. It's no wonder she became the outstanding Hindi-speaker of us all."

Each student had private language sessions with a pundit—an Indian teacher. Anna met with her pundit from four to five o'clock every afternoon.

The pundit wore a straight piece of cloth wound around his body to make loose trousers. He kept his hair short except one six-inch lock on top that he tied into a little knot that hung down. By this, everyone recognized him as a Hindu who believed someone would pull him to heaven by his lock of hair.

One week, Anna's pundit did not come to language study for two days. "I know his baby has been sick," she said. "I'll go see if I can help the family."

When Anna entered the two cluttered and drab rooms, she discovered the teacher had gone on an errand. His wife, however, sat anxiously beside the poorly clothed, sick baby. Anna thought of the correct Hindi words and asked, "May I help you?"

The frightened mother explained she hadn't slept for four days. "I'm too worried to sleep," she said.

"If you want me to come to sit with the baby tonight so you can sleep, let me know," said Anna.

"Yes," replied the mother.

Anna heard about the baby's death a few days later. When her pundit returned to language study, he said, "I'm so sorry I was out buying medicine for our baby when you came. I should have been there to serve tea to you. I thought about calling you to come sit with the baby that night. I knew, though, my wife would stay up anyway, so you wouldn't really need to come." He wiped his eyes, swollen from crying and lack of sleep.

Studying came hard for Anna that day. The thin pundit didn't have much strength to teach, either.

The next week he said, "You have been so kind, please come to our house for tea."

"I'll be glad to come," Anna replied.

This time the tiny house looked clean. A cloth covered the table. The pundit and his wife served tea, delicious Indian sweets, roasted corn, and a special treat called Dal Mote. *This looks almost like peanuts*, Anna thought. The flavor, however, made her think of a roaring fire.

* * *

As often as possible, Anna spoke Hindi to the Indian people. She tried to understand their customs. It took a while to learn about the levels of society called castes. The entire way of life for an Indian family depended upon whether it belonged to the high caste, low caste, outcaste, or some level in between.

"There's no way an Indian can change caste, either," Norma said to Anna. "Everyone is born into a caste and must always stay in that specific one."

*   *   *

"Anna," said Alena Calkins, "my vacation's done, and I'm headed back to Chhatarpur. I'm going to stop at Kaimganj (Kimeguns) to visit Indian friends. Why don't you go with me? The day and night on the train will be a chance for you to see more of India."

Anna agreed to go.

A few days later, Anna and Alena climbed aboard the train. They found sitting space in the women's compartment. They arranged their food, drinking water, and bedding beside their feet as the Indian women stared at them. "We're the only foreigners in here," Anna whispered to Alena.

Anna especially noticed the young Indian woman who wore a gold sari trimmed with real silver thread. She had a star painted on her forehead. A streak of red paint decorated the part in her black hair. Red paint also covered the palms of her hands. The side of her nose held a sparkling jewel. More jewels swung back and forth from her ears and a ring circled each finger. Several toes had rings on them, also. Anna took time to count the forty bracelets on the young woman's arms.

Heavy golden ankle-rings jangled as the young woman moved to get closer to Anna. "I know how to speak your language," the Indian said softly in perfect English. "I attended a mission school."

Later in their conversation, Anna found out the woman had also read the Bible. *I want Christianity to reach her heart, not just her mind*, thought Anna. *Here's a need for prayer.* As it would often happen in the years to come, Anna never knew the answer to that prayer.

More and more women pushed their way into the compartment each time the train stopped. Some of them looked like ghosts in their heavy *burkahs*. These cloaks entirely covered their bodies. Upon getting settled, they turned back the *burkahs* and Anna could see the beautiful faces. She also saw old and ugly faces. The minute the train stopped at the next station, all of them quickly hid themselves in their *burkahs*. Once again they all looked alike.

At one station, a cart covered with red print material stopped beside the train. Anna heard loud wails. Well-dressed people who carried bright bouquets and noisemakers gathered around.

"It's a wedding party," Alena said.

Several people reached inside the cart and pulled out the young girl, who still wailed. She nearly fell onto the train as the others pushed her inside. No one acted concerned about her calls for help.

"She's the bride," Alena explained to Anna. "The other woman with her would be her mother-in-law." The train jerked into motion again while the sobbing bride sat with her red sari pulled well over her face.

"Is she really so sad?" Anna asked Alena.

"Probably she's partly sad. It's also the custom for brides to act that way."

Anna prayed for the bride. *I wish these women of India knew about God and His happiness*, she thought.

Anna saw more sad sights at each train station. She felt helpless in the middle of so much suffering and hardship. Once, a sick-looking, noseless beggar peered into their window. The missionaries gave some of their lunch to him.

When Anna and Alena reached Kaimganj, the Chaturvedi family gave them a kind welcome. Many servants made sure the tired women had everything they needed. *What luxury!* thought Anna. *It's so different from all we saw on the train.*

Anna worried that she might do the wrong thing. "Their customs are so different," she said to Alena. "I'm glad you're here to help me know what to do." The missionaries dressed in Indian clothes and ate Indian food. They became friends with the Chaturvedi children.

The time passed quickly and soon Anna and Alena prepared to leave this fine high-caste Hindu home. One of the little servant girls tugged at

Anna's hand to pull her back. Anna knelt down and wrapped her arms around the child.

Later Anna said, "It didn't matter that crusty scabs covered her body. I loved her, anyway. I want her and all the other children of India to know Jesus who loves every boy and girl."

*   *   *

July 25, 1946

Dear Mother and Dad,

Our customs are so different from Indian customs. Yet, as I come to know these wonderful people, I find we all have the same need for Jesus Christ, our Savior.

Love,
Anna

*   *   *

The weeks at language school came to an end, and Anna passed the examinations with high grades. Immediately she headed down the hill away from Landour and toward the plains of Bundelkhand, the area in central India containing the Friends Mission.

"At last I'm ready to get to work," she said.

Chapter 6

DIVING RIGHT IN

As soon as Anna settled into the mission house in Chhatarpur, she began to get acquainted. Right away she felt concerned for the Hindu children in her neighborhood.

"They don't want to go to Sunday school at the church," she said. She soon organized a class for them that met on the porch in front of her house. During the week, Anna showed several Indian women how to tell the Bible story for the next Sunday school session. She sat among the children on Sundays while the Indian teachers told the stories and led in worship.

Only children from Christian families attended this Sunday school at first. Gradually, a few others came to visit. Then, one Sunday, fifty boys and girls showed up, most coming from Hindu homes. They wore rings in their noses, around their ankles, on their wrists, and in their ears. Grimy rags covered their bodies, which smelled of dirt and sores. They continued to come, anxious to

41

receive the greeting card pictures the teachers handed out every fourth Sunday.

As Christmas drew near, Anna told Alena, "I must write a drama so the children can present the true Christmas message. Many people who don't know anything about Jesus' birth or why He came to earth will be here for the program."

The children all wanted to have a part. Little shepherds, angels, wise men, and a small Mary and Joseph diligently practiced the important drama. On December 22, entire families came to watch the story of Jesus' birth. Anna prayed for these people who had never seen or heard anything like it before.

*   *   *

"One of the head teachers at our school in Nowgong is sick. Anna, we need you to fill in," said one of the missionaries in January, 1947.

A few months later, the mission council appointed her to be in charge of the Nowgong Christian School.

"The idea of such a responsible job scares me," Anna admitted. "But I see I am to do it."

She dived right into arranging schedules, getting books for the students, and hiring teachers. Her job even included overseeing the school gardens. Since she had to make sure everything about the school happened as it should, Anna sometimes thought she would never catch up with herself.

The second year things became easier when she hired a good headmistress. That year Anna suggested the children could work a few hours a week at school to earn spending money.

The children groaned. "We don't want to work," they said. "Work is for poor and uneducated people."

"After all, we're educated," one boy pointed out. "We're in the fourth class now."

Anna continued talking about the work idea. After much discussion both for and against, the plan went into effect.

On October 29, Anna's birthday, the school children surprised her with a program and gifts. "Now please let us have a holiday," they said.

"A holiday?" laughed Anna. "No, we must continue with classes."

The boys and girls coaxed. "We have holidays for celebrating birthdays of great people."

Anna laughed again. "Thank you for the compliment. I'm not that great, though."

* * *

One Tuesday morning soon after revival meetings, Anna noticed how solemn her students looked. "Perhaps we should pray," she suggested.

After the prayer, Anna opened her eyes and discovered half of the class had disappeared. "They've gone to ask forgiveness," a girl explained.

One by one the missing students came back. The group prayed again, then several children tiptoed around the room. They whispered to one another, asking forgiveness. One boy confessed to Anna that he needed to pay a shopkeeper for things he had stolen. Others said they would return items they had taken from the missionaries.

Anna noticed a little Hindu girl sitting at her desk, quietly watching and listening. "You can pray if you want to," Anna said.

Tears ran down the little girl's face and splashed off her chin. "I want to," she replied, "but I don't know how."

Anna knelt beside her. "You can tell God what you want to," she said. "Would you like me to help you?"

The girl nodded. Anna helped her ask God to forgive her sin and to give her peace. Then she offered, "I'll be glad to go home with you when you tell your mother and father." Anna hoped they would not punish their daughter for becoming a Christian.

Anna walked home with the little girl after school. Her parents hardly knew what to do. They listened, however, as she told them, "I prayed in the name of Jesus. Now I have peace in my heart."

The girl came back to school the next morning. The big smile on her shining brown face made Anna say, "Thank You, Lord."

*   *   *

"I wish more villagers would decide to become Christians," Anna said sadly. "Some say they want to be Christians, but so few actually go ahead and leave their old ways behind." She knew that in order to live as Christians, the Indian people had to change their ways of doing everything.

Soon, certain village Indians quietly told Anna and the other missionaries, "We are Christians now. We're afraid, though, that others will persecute us." Some prayed for God to take the evil spirits out of their lives. One man asked help to stop smoking the deadly drug, opium.

"Our work takes a lot of faith, but I wouldn't trade jobs with anyone," Anna told another missionary. "We're in the greatest work in the world!"

The missionaries continued to pray. Six more village families became Christians before long.

"It's wonderful to see the Lord working with them," said Anna. "But these new Christians have never had a chance to know how to read or write."

*   *   *

May 9, 1949

Dear Mother and Dad,

We're going now to the mountains of South India to get away from the heat. It would be too hard on our health to stick through the hot season (temperatures up to 120 degrees) without a break.

Love,
Anna

45

Vacations always meant a long trip by train to the hills of South India or to the beautiful mountains at Landour. Most times, some of the missionaries Anna had known in prison showed up at the same place. They got together to eat hot fudge sundaes and chat about things of interest to all. They attended weekly tea gatherings where Anna met many others who became lifetime friends. On cool evenings they all visited together in front of a snapping fire in the fireplace.

Anna knitted, read books, entertained guests, sang in a choir, and relaxed with extra sleep. The beautiful flowers, trees, and mountains made her feel refreshed. Sometimes she took work along, doing her best to make time to write or plan the year ahead.

Anna liked having missionary children come to visit for an hour, a day, or longer. They all loved their Auntie Anna as much as she loved them. Once three little girls who stayed four days called her Auntie Banana. She nicknamed them Cherry, Plum, and Peach. "We're the Fruit family," giggled the girls.

At another vacation time, Carol Coleman, Milton and Rebecca's daughter, came to Anna's door early one Saturday morning, "Some of us want to go on a picnic today. Will you take us, Auntie?"

"Sure," Anna quickly agreed. "I'll get the lunch ready while you choose the place."

Anna gasped as they began their hike. "This path goes straight up the mountain," she said. She stopped and panted after several minutes of climbing. "You girls dash up the hillside like mountain goats, but I'm not made for a climb like this."

"Never mind, Auntie," Carol said. "I'll take you by another path. It's easier." She headed downward.

Anna's right foot slipped. Her left foot did, too. She grabbed at tree roots and rocks as she slid to a safe landing. Then she straightened up to follow Carol, who had already started up another leafy path. Anna placed one foot slowly and carefully in front of the other. Her hands clung to the side of the cliff. She peeked sideways at the valley far below. *If my foot slips on these leaves, I'll end up down there in a hurry,* she thought.

"Don't be afraid, Auntie, and you won't fall," Carol called out cheerfully as she sprinted along.

At last the girls announced, "Here we are. This is our picnic spot."

Never again, thought Anna.

*　　*　　*

Whether on vacation or not, Anna always welcomed news from home. She felt close to family and friends with every letter and package that came. Anna wrote many letters herself.

She could always write detailed, interesting letters on the typewriter or by hand. It didn't matter where she happened to be at the time. Sometimes her suitcase served as a desk as she wrote letters in a crowded train station. At other times she wrote while riding on the rattling, swaying train itself or while sitting up in bed at home.

Once she answered letters as she sat in the shade of a big tree alongside the river. *The wind must die down before the rickety ferry can take me across,* she wrote.

*   *   *

In 1950, Anna moved back to Chhatarpur from Nowgong.

Once again she took on several jobs. She supervised the nurses' home next to the mission hospital while also working in the mission office. Sunday school work for the entire mission came under Anna's direction, too.

In her spare time, she began to develop proper materials for the village Sunday schools. First Anna wrote the outline, did the lessons in English, and then translated them into Hindi. She had no idea this would be important for a mission assignment yet to come.

The years went by quickly, and Anna made plans to return to the United States for furlough. "I will come back," she said. "I can see God working with the Indian people. I can't think of anyplace I would rather be."

She visited her family and friends in Colorado and elsewhere. Many church people invited her to speak about her work. The next time Anna saw India, in the fall of 1953, she found a whole new set of opportunities.

Chapter 7

THREE PILLS AT ONCE

"We're going out into the villages soon," Catherine Cattell, another Friends missionary, told Anna after she returned to India. "It would be a good opportunity for you to go with us."

Anna liked the idea and began to prepare for the stay in the country. "I'll have to learn the village dialect," she said.

The missionaries and Indian workers went first to a village 38 miles from Chhatarpur. They set up four tents (two for men and two for women) where they could sleep inside on the cold nights.

During the days, Anna went along to help Catherine with classes.* Anna played the organ-like harmonium as Catherine led the singing. She also placed the figures on the flannelgraph board when Catherine told Bible stories.

Anna watched the people closely while they sat on the ground under the trees listening to

* Read more about Catherine Cattell in Happiness Under the Indian Trees, also by Betty M. Hockett.

Catherine. *They're so interested,* she thought. *They seem to take hold of what we teach them. I believe they recognize the truth. If only they will determine to follow God's way.*

One morning Anna and Catherine came upon a distressed woman standing in the alley. "There they are!" she cried. "They're the ones!" She pointed a skinny brown finger at Anna and Catherine. "What kind of magic have you worked on my son? He says he will stay with me only a short while longer. Then he will leave me to become a Christian. He's all I have. When he goes how will I eat?"

The missionaries tried to comfort the woman. "Why do you accuse us? We don't teach that your son should dishonor and disobey his mother. Haven't you heard us say that when you become a Christian you should stay in your same house and village and keep on with your same work? We haven't asked anyone to leave this village. We only say, 'Leave your sins.' "

Others leaned against the trees beside the dusty alley. "What the white women say is right," someone said.

The crying mother wiped her eyes. "Then you will not take my son away from me?"

"We have no desire to take your son from you," Anna said. The woman slowly walked away, smiling instead of weeping.

Many of the people, like this mother, knew nothing about Christianity. As they gathered under the trees each day, Anna gladly told them how Jesus wanted to forgive them. Sometimes, though, she decided the people didn't really hear or want to make changes in their lives. "We must try, though, and the camping program seems the best way," she said.

Anna quickly adapted to the outdoor village camp life. She wrapped, twisted and folded six yards of fabric around her body to create a sari like the Indian women wore. Eating the same food her Indian co-workers ate agreed with her.

Dust and inconveniences didn't matter when courageous villagers said, "We want to believe in Jesus Christ. We will worship only Him." Then Anna would think, *This makes it worth all the effort.*

The diseases, sore eyes, and blindness that afflicted so many country people made Anna wish she could help. "They're so used to living this way they don't want to bother taking medicines," Catherine said. "Besides, they believe evil spirits cause disease. They don't know anything about germs."

Once Anna wanted to give three pills to a sick boy. "This medicine will help your son get over the malaria attack," she told the Indian mother.

Immediately the mother cried angrily, "You're trying to kill my son! Whoever heard of taking three pills at once." She held the boy tightly against her. "Besides, these pills cost three coins each. I know there are plenty of pills that only cost one coin. Just give us some of those."

Even though Anna tried to explain, the mother wouldn't agree to giving her son three pills at one time.

At a later time, in another village, Anna and an Indian co-worker, Virginia Singh, taught about good health practices. They set up their flannel-graph board and told their story about smallpox. "This is Gore Bai," said Anna, putting an Indian figure on the board. "She wouldn't let the doctor give her a smallpox vaccination. What do you think happened to her?"

At that moment a gust of wind blew the Gore Bai figure off the board. Everyone laughed as it landed on the ground. A loud voice shouted, "I know what happened to her. She fell down!"

The next day Anna and Virginia showed a filmstrip that demonstrated how to care for sore eyes. Soon after, a mother brought her child to these two Christian workers. Pus oozed from underneath the boy's red, swollen eyelids. Anna gently washed his eyes. Virginia then helped the mother understand how she could do the same treatment at home.

"See, we're doing it exactly as you saw in the pictures," Anna explained.

"I'm glad you have come to help us," the Indian mother said. Later Anna heard how other mothers in that village had done the right things for their children's sore eyes, too.

"This gives us hope," Anna said. "Some days I feel more and more hopeless up against the poverty, ignorance and superstition, running sores, filth, and flies. Today, however, I feel hopeful."

*   *   *

June 1955

Dear Mother and Dad,

I'm on vacation in the hills now because the temperature on the plains is up to 116 degrees. I'm writing a novel called, *More Than Shadow*. It's about an Indian boy, and I'm having heaps of fun doing it. I will enter it in a writing contest.

Love,
Anna

*   *   *

"I want to help the Indian village women learn to read," said Anna. "I'm going to begin classes for them."

One or two women acted interested. Others hung back when relatives made fun of them. "It's almost too much for them," Anna said. "They want to learn a lot without any effort. They've never had to learn things like this before."

Sometimes, though, the women couldn't take time to come to reading classes. They had too much work in their fields. Anna kept on trying, hoping more women would learn to read.

Then, at last, she handed out the first reading certificate ever given by Friends missionaries in Bundelkhand. By that time, four more women and two men had started the reading course. Others said they would come after harvest time.

The next week, Colemans brought a letter to Anna.

"Hmmm! This looks important," she said. "I wonder what it is."

Anna teaching an Indian girl to read

Chapter 8

CLOSE TO TROUBLE

Anna quickly opened the envelope.

"It's from the Evangelical Fellowship of India," she told Milton and Rebecca. "The letter says, 'We are glad to tell you that you are the second-place winner of the novel contest. We will publish your book, *More Than Shadow*, in English and then translate and publish it in Hindi next year.' "

Anna smiled. "I'm pleased and surprised, too. I really didn't expect they would publish it. I just wanted to write about real life here in our area of India." At that time Anna had no idea her book would later appear in six more languages, or that the All-India Christian Book Club would select it for its readers.

*   *   *

By the beginning of 1956, nine Indian people had enrolled in Anna's reading program. Others came nearly every day asking, "Can we learn to read, too?" Anna felt glad to see some results in that part

55

of the mission work. "We're up against great difficulties in India," she said. "Little by little, though, we can see God at work among the people."

She patiently listened to beginning readers blunder through the sentences during reading classes. One day an Indian woman reached out to touch Anna's hair. "How fine it is," she said, twirling her fingers through her own twisted and matted hair.

Someone else pulled at Anna's stocking that showed beneath her sari. "Sister, I wish you would make us like you are."

Whatever does she mean? Anna wondered. *They've just been talking about how odd I look.*

Others began to answer. "She means she wants to be a white person like you ... She wants to be a Christian ... No, she means she wants to be educated like you."

"Exactly what do you mean?" Anna asked.

The Indian woman answered. "I mean I want to be like you so I can sit all day and do nothing and eat good food and live in a nice house."

Anna groaned to herself. *Do nothing, like me? With my days always full and rushed?* Then she thought, *My Indian sister here has full days, too. She plasters the floor of her house with cow dung, grinds the grain, gathers wood, and carries water from the well. She also makes the bread, washes her sari, and cares for the children. Probably she goes out to the field to earn a day's wages, besides.*

Anna explained about her own work. Then she said, "My sister in America works hard. My parents also work hard."

The next day she told Catherine, "The Indian women didn't understand at all."

* * *

A few months later, Anna moved to Jhansi. There, she took on a whole new job, the start of her work with the Evangelical Fellowship of India.

That first year in Jhansi she lived in a house on a hill that gave her a lovely view all around. Many colorful plants added their beauty to the house and grounds. Since the mission house had plenty of space (twenty rooms and big hallways), other missionaries sometimes came to live there, too.

Being in the EFI office helped Anna become acquainted with many mission groups and churches who cooperated in several projects. Some workers prepared programs for a daily three-hour radio broadcast. Others helped teach Christian leaders and pastors throughout India.

"We have a big job to do," Anna said. "The literature work especially appeals to me, though." She longed for the Indian people to have better Christian reading and study materials.

As usual, Anna had more than enough to do. Stacks of letters arrived at the office, and she had to answer them. She also organized and planned conferences, then wrote reports about them later. Sometimes she accepted speaking engagements, too. On top of everything else, she agreed to be the secretary for the Missionary Language School. "I'll be in charge of the centers where people come for the exams," she explained.

Anna's job soon included the All-India Christian Book Club. Church leaders asked her, also, to look at Christian education in India. "We want to know what you think needs to be done," they said.

Anna and others who helped make the survey discovered that only a few Indian churches had Sunday schools. They also reported, "There are no complete Sunday school materials in any Indian language."

Everyone knew it would take thousands of dollars to write, translate, and publish books for Indian Sunday schools. Sadly they admitted, "There's no money to do such a big job for all of India." They dropped the idea for the moment.

Almost before she knew it, Anna's first year at the Evangelical Fellowship office had passed. "I'm quite content with life and have plenty to keep me busy," she said.

She moved from the house on the hill to a not-so-nice building. It, too, contained plenty of room for guests. Gladys Jasper and her dog named Lady arrived, then stayed on while Gladys worked with Anna in the EFI office.

Short-term guests from many missions came and went at a constant pace. Sometimes the house almost overflowed with people. "I feel good when my house is full," Anna said.

She often hurried to the train station to meet a missionary friend coming or going through Jhansi. Sometimes that meant a quick visit at the station with Anna furnishing a cold or hot drink for the traveler. At other times she took the friend home for tea or a meal.

Anna readily comforted co-workers who received sad news from home. She took care of missionary children while their parents were sick or away. Staff members knew from experience that Anna would gladly help out if they fell ill. One of her Indian assistants said, "Anna takes good care of my family when I go on tour. She has great sympathy for us and always tries to encourage us."

Anna had a hard time finding good cooks. "If I don't have a cook," she explained, "I don't get anything done but cook, especially with so many guests."

One cook turned out to be dishonest. Anna dismissed him. Another kept saying, "I can't do that." He stood around, refusing to learn.

"He may not stay long either," said Anna.

Then she found just the right cook. He worked quickly, and the food he prepared tasted good. Late one afternoon Anna unexpectedly invited a missionary family to stay overnight. She hurried to the kitchen to tell the cook, "Please prepare food for six. I'll be back as soon as I take a friend to the train."

When Anna returned, she went to see what the cook had fixed on such short notice. She saw only an ugly hash of meat and rice. *Oh, dear,* she thought. *I'm embarrassed to serve this horrid mess to guests. I'd better say it kindly, though.*

Anna smiled at the cook and said as gently as possible, "Perhaps we should open some tins of tuna."

"Oh, this rice and meat is for the dog your guests brought along," the cook replied. He pointed to three pans covered with lids. "There's plenty of good food in those."

* * *

Anna often rode on the bumpy Indian trains in order to do EFI business in other areas of the country. At the start of one such trip, she came close to trouble.

She paid for her ticket while watching the train pull in on the far tracks beyond a long bridge. Then she gathered her purse between two small leather bags in her left hand and lifted her heavy suitcase with her right hand.

After only a few steps she realized she couldn't carry the heavy suitcase. Anna looked out among the people swarming around, waiting for trains. Suddenly she spotted the red coat of a coolie. As he looked her direction, she motioned for him to carry her suitcase and follow her.

Reaching the train, Anna pulled herself up the steep steps and put down her bags. The coolie, right behind her, set the suitcase on the floor and held his hand out for pay. Anna reached for her purse. "It's gone!" she exclaimed. "My purse is gone! I had it in my hand!" Panic swept over her. "My money – my passport – my permit to live in India! Everything's in my purse. What should I do?"

"I saw a black bag on the platform over across the tracks when I picked up your suitcase," the coolie replied.

"Oh, please wait here!" Anna ordered. She jumped off the train to run, puffing and praying, back over the bridge. Then she saw it! Her purse lay on the platform in a big empty circle. Hundreds of people milled about as if the purse had been invisible.

Anna grabbed the purse and rushed back to the train. She handed the coolie an especially generous tip as the train slowly began to steam out of the station.

*   *   *

April 3, 1958

Dear Mother and Dad,

I'm about to get involved in a project that will take all my time for several years. I will need help for I cannot do it by myself.

Love,
Anna

At last the time had come. It would, however, turn out to be a bigger job than Anna ever dreamed.

Landour •

New
Delhi ★

Kaimgang •
Jhansi •
Nowgong • • • Chhatarpur
Gulganj •
BUNDELKHAND

Calcutta •

• Yavatmal

Bombay •
• Pune

INDIA

Madras •

Chapter 9

FITTING IT ALL TOGETHER

"It will be a tremendous job to develop the Sunday schools of India and produce materials for them," said Anna. "After all, we need lessons in six or eight languages."

Anna worked hard to organize the task. To begin with, she searched for Sunday school materials appropriate for India. Then she found people to rewrite the books and afterward translate them into Indian languages. She discovered a missionary nurse, also an artist, who said she would draw the pictures.

Anna made arrangements for printers in Calcutta to publish the books. An important part of the task involved contacting people in the United States who had said they would pay for this Christian education work.

Being in charge of this big job, Anna edited all of the Sunday school books. This meant she had to read everything the others wrote. Then, if necessary, she made changes in order for every lesson to be correct. Occasionally she wrote some of the lessons herself.

Five people helped her at the beginning. Then others said they would join in. Anna trained Indian Christians, too. "After a while they'll be able to take more of the responsibility," she said.

Anna fit this work into the coming years. Sometimes she asked, "Why did I ever think I could even try to do this job? It's too big!" Quickly she would remind herself, *I am here because God wanted me in this place at this time for this job.*

Interest in the Christian education program grew. People in Africa, Taiwan, United States, England, and India wrote to Anna. She carefully answered their questions about the Sunday school materials.

At last Anna and her assistants completed the first Sunday school course. They all sang, "Praise God from whom all blessings flow."

"We couldn't do it without Him," Anna said. "This material printed in India's own language is the first of its kind. I never dreamed, though, it would take so much work."

Sometime later, they finished the second course. Anna wrapped the bundle of manuscript papers. "We should send this to the printer right away," she said as she shook her head sadly. "But there's not enough money to have it printed now." She finished getting the package ready, anyway. Then Anna led the way to the noon prayer meeting that had become the daily custom before lunch.

When she arrived back at the office later, Anna received the mail for the day. She saw the publisher's name on the first letter she opened. He had written, *Send the next course right away. Money has come to begin the publication.*

"Thank the Lord!" Anna exclaimed and immediately sent the package on its way to the publisher.

The staff faced the same problem when they completed the next course. "Come look!" Anna called when she opened a letter that day. "God has done it again. The daffodil man has sent another $1,000."

"The who?" asked the typist.

"The daffodil man—Mr. Willard Pim. He lives in Ohio. Every year he plants hundreds of daffodil bulbs. In the spring he sells the blooms and gives the money to missions. God knew we needed Mr. Pim's check today."

Before he died, Mr. Pim had sent a total of $15,000 from his daffodil sales. His money paid for printing 75,000 books for the Sunday schools of India.

Anna kept busy preparing the next courses. Pastors sent word, "We want help for our Sunday schools." Anna and other teacher-trainers traveled to these churches. They showed teachers how to use the new Sunday school materials.

"We're glad for your help," the teachers said. "This is the first time we've had books for us and for our students, too."

* * *

June 15, 1963

Dear Mother and Dad,

My work keeps growing like a spring flower in the warm sun. But I can truthfully say, I've never done anything I enjoyed so much.

Love,
Anna

*   *   *

More and more people wanted to know about the Christian education program of the Evangelical Fellowship of India. Anna, and others as well, referred to the program as CEEFI. This growing interest often sent Anna aboard the train for work-travel.

Almost always the train cars overflowed with tired adults and screaming children. Sometimes Anna had to wedge herself, her jug of drinking water, her food, and a roll of blankets in between *burkah*-clad mothers and their dirty children. At other times she couldn't find any place to sit. If the train didn't jerk and bump too much, Anna used the travel time to write letters or lessons.

She bumped along from committee meeting to committee meeting or from conference to conference where she told large audiences about CEEFI. These hot, dusty, smoky trips aboard the noisy, bumpy trains, also took Anna to see writers and printers. She sometimes visited book shops and mission stations. Some trips kept her away from home for weeks at a time.

On one 2,000-mile trip, she spent six nights on the train or in the waiting rooms of train stations. "I got a lot of business done, but I'm awfully glad to be home again," she told friends.

Once she reported, "It has taken most of my time this last month to wait for the trains to move. Of course I spent the rest of my time washing the soot out of my nose and hair as well as off my hands and face. Traveling makes me feel tired, but it gets me in touch with a lot of interesting places and people."

At last Anna had the opportunity to ride in a new kind of train car. For sixty cents she rented a padded bench perched above the long, bare board seats. That night she put a bedspread brought from home over the padded bench. She placed her foam rubber pillow at one end of the rented bench and slept until the next morning. She got to her destination the morning after that. "I've had two good nights of sleep on this train," she said.

Several years later, Anna had a happy surprise. "I've discovered a new fast train that goes only between Delhi and Calcutta," she said. "They serve meals on the train, just like in a plane. I had a smooth ride in an air-conditioned coach equipped with comfortable seats. I hope they'll soon get more trains like this in India. Travel then would be quite a treat."

*   *   *

On November 19, 1965, at 3:30 in the afternoon, Anna announced joyfully, "We've finished the last Sunday school course. That means God has helped us prepare fifteen different books for teachers and sixty different books for students."

She looked at the tall stacks of books for young children, middle-sized boys and girls, teenagers, and grownups. "Sometimes the work we had to do seemed like a high mountain we could never get over. God helped us, though. Now the Sunday schools of India and in other places, too, can have Bible lesson books every week."

Three years later, Anna discovered another need. "Youth workers don't have any books to help them teach their young people," she said. Anna and her team got busy on this new project. When they finished, someone else translated the 48 lessons into Indian languages.

Youth workers thanked Anna. "We're happy to have these lesson books," they said. "They're something entirely new for India."

Anna gradually turned some of the work of CEEFI over to others. Writers had translated the Sunday school materials into 16 languages. Vacation Bible schools and teacher training sessions continued to grow. Youth workers kept on ordering lesson books.

Anna had more and more invitations to speak at conferences. She worked hard to help church leaders know how they could have good Sunday schools. People all over the world watched Christian education in India.

*   *   *

The time had come again for Anna to return to the United States. As she prepared to leave, a telephone call came to her one night. She struggled for more than an hour to hear the voice at the other end of the line. Finally she heard, "Father just died. Can you come?"

People who worked with Anna assured her, "Don't worry. We'll take care of things here." They helped complete Anna's work so she could leave earlier than planned. "It's important for you to go home to comfort your mother," her friends said.

*   *   *

The next year, Malone College in Ohio honored Anna with a Doctor of Literature degree. Everett Cattell, president of the college, said, "Anna, you have won the respect and admiration of all who know you. We're proud of you. We thank God for what He has accomplished through you. You deserve to be honored." He also spoke of experiences he and his wife, Catherine, had shared with Anna in India.

"Thank you," replied Anna. "I didn't really see the necessity of this degree, but for me to have it means a lot to many people."

A month later, Anna returned to India for the fifth time.

*   *   *

69

May 1973

Dear Mother,

I'm going to be doing something I never thought I would do. I will teach Christian education and English in the Union Biblical Seminary in Yavatmal, India. Students come from all over Asia and Africa and from every state in India. It's a privilege for me to be here in India.

Love,
Anna

Fannie Nixon, Anna's mother, did not receive that letter. She had already gone to heaven before it arrived.

* * *

Anna taught at the seminary for seven years. Then something unexpected occurred that made her uncertain about what would happen next.

१६ क्योंकि परमेश्वर ने जगत मे ऐसा प्रेम ग्वा कि उम ने म्रपना एकलौता पुत्र दे दिया, नाकि जो कोई उम पर विश्वाम करे, वह नाश न हो, परन्तु म्रनन्त जीवन पाए । यूहन्ना ३ : १६

John 3:16 written in Hindi

Chapter 10

WHAT'S NEXT, LORD?

"Anna," said the mission doctor, "you haven't felt well for several months even though you've tried to work. You need more medical help than we can give you here. I advise you to go back to the United States for at least six months."

Anna sat quietly with her fingers clutched together. Her good health had been a blessing these years in India. Only minor upsets had caused her to take a few days off now and then.

At last she answered softly, "Yes, I had hoped to continue in India. But you're probably right, Doctor. I'll leave as soon as I can."

Anna had appointment after appointment with different doctors in the United States. Close friends did all they could. "I'm overcome by the love you have shown to me," she said.

Anna still felt miserable. She continually wondered what would happen next. Even so, she truthfully sang, "'Tis so sweet to trust in Jesus."

As time went on, she began to feel better. She visited churches whose members had been faithful to remember her through the years. "Thank you for the letters and packages you sent to me in India," she said. "I knew you loved me and prayed for me. Your encouragement brightened my days many times."

One day the phone rang. The caller said, "Anna, we want to give you an honorary doctorate here at Friends University."

After praying about it, Anna felt she should accept this new honor. "God may use this in some way for His glory," she said.

A few months later she felt well enough to return to India.

Anna tried to once again keep a full schedule. She soon realized, however, she couldn't continue. A few weeks later she said final good-byes to India and its people. "I must go," she said. "This time had to come, but it won't be easy."

*   *   *

Back in Ohio again, Anna saw one doctor after another. Unfortunately they weren't able to help her. As she read her Bible and prayed every day, God blessed her with promises from the Scriptures. She also read books, hoping to find answers to questions about her health. Anna felt determined to trust God for whatever would be ahead.

As she felt able, Anna worked on a writing project she had started before leaving India. "I really want to finish this history of our American Friends Mission in India," she said.

After a time, God helped Anna find the right doctor. He prescribed appropriate medicine that helped her feel better day by day. Now she could think about the future, although she knew she would not return to India.

She decided to move to Friendsview Manor in Newberg, Oregon. When Anna arrived, Catherine Cattell rushed out to meet her. She led the way to room 224, Anna's new home. Anna enjoyed seeing many who had prayed for her while she had been in India. She quickly made many new friends, too.

Her health remained good, and she got the history of the Indian mission off to the printers. Soon she announced, "I'm going to Bolivia to teach English in the Evangelical University there. Afterward I'll come home by way of Holland, India, and Australia."

Anna's first sight of Santa Cruz reminded her of cities in India. Traffic rushed for the right of way at every intersection in that large and busy Bolivian city. Mobs of pedestrians cluttered streets and sidewalks. Children and dogs ran freely among curious buyers who carried baskets.

Anna's classes got off to a slow and uncertain beginning. Strikes, lights going out, traffic jams, and conflicts in class schedules caused problems. Little by little, though, everything smoothed out.

*   *   *

December 1, 1984

Dear Friends,

We finished classes and the students now take their exams. I look forward to Christmas in Holland and a different kind of work in an office for two or three months with Gladys Jasper.

Sincerely,

Anna

Anna spent several weeks helping Gladys. Then she headed to India by way of The Netherlands.

Upon arriving in India, she visited the Union Biblical Seminary campus, newly located in Pune. The trip included stops in Chhatarpur, Hyderabad, Jhansi, Yavatmal, and other places where she had lived and worked. Anna accepted invitations to participate in several services. While in India, she wrote another book, *Dr. Grace of Bundelkhand*, the story of an Indian medical doctor who worked at the mission hospital.

Anna heard reports in India that made her glad. More Sunday schools than ever used the printed materials Anna helped to develop through CEEFI. "They're available in 26 languages now," a worker told her. "Churches in some African countries use them, too."

Leaving India, Anna traveled to Australia to visit friends before going home to Oregon.

Later that summer many people bought *A Century of Planting*, the book Anna had written about the Friends mission in India. Then Anna began to ask once more, "What's next, Lord?"

It didn't take long for the answer to come: write another book. This time she would write about Ezra and Frances DeVol, missionaries she had worked with in India. This book, *On the Cutting Edge*, pleased readers.

Anna kept on writing, even as she asked again, "What's next, Lord?"

She waited for the answer, filling in as church secretary for a few weeks. She also volunteered to help in the Friendsview Manor health care center.

Sunday school teaching and church missionary committee meetings took up many hours every week. Still full of energy, creativity, and imagination, Anna enrolled in a class at George Fox College.

Sometimes Anna wondered, *Am I doing the most important things?* She always reminded herself, *I try to do those things which will be a help to people.*

Long days and nights on the train had mostly become memories for Anna. "I've seldom traveled just for the sake of traveling," she explained. "Travels have been a part of my ministry and service to the Lord." This continued to be true. Anna drove her car or traveled by bus or plane to conferences where she told about her missionary work.

In the spring of 1989, Anna planned one more long cross-country trip by train. "I'm going mainly to attend the 28th reunion of my graduation from

Friends University and also the 50th reunion of my class at Malone College. After those events I'll visit special Indian friends in Boston and Washington D.C. I'll also go on to see Milton and Rebecca Coleman in Florida."

At the Malone reunion, college officials honored Anna by naming her the "Alumnus of the Year."

"This special trip has inspired and blessed me," Anna said when she arrived back at Friendsview Manor.

Meanwhile, from north to south in India and in Africa, too, the work Anna did to help others goes on and on. To this day, many praise Anna and thank her for what she did through CEEFI.

"She saw what the churches of India needed," former co-workers readily say. "Then she willingly worked hard to provide them with materials and instruction. Anna's total commitment, compassion, and love have changed the lives of countless children and adults."

As long as her strength lasts, Anna will continue to help in the work of the church, to write, and to entertain guests. She will do all she can to help others while asking herself and God, "What's next?"